Mother of the Groom

By

Jane Sabatino

ISBN: 1-4107-0444-0 (e-book)
ISBN: 1-4107-0445-9 (Paperback)

Library of Congress Control Number: 2002096611

This book is printed on acid free paper.

Printed in the United States of America
Bloomington, IN

1stBooks – rev. 01/22/03

TABLE OF CONTENTS

PREFACE

I have two wonderful sons. There is a three year difference in their ages. But their weddings were only two years apart. So I spent two recent years planning for and attending two important events in our lives. I survived both their weddings, but it was not easy.

I have always been the type of person who learned things the hard way. I would not listen to the advice of my parents or well meaning friends. Therefore, I have made many mistakes in my life. So it was with my sons' weddings. I learned enough through the experiences that I hope I never have to go through this again. But if I do, I will know how to dress, act, and react to whatever comes along.

Like most mothers who adore their sons, I had planned for their weddings in my mind for years. But when it came time to actually get ready, I was ill prepared. I read as many magazines and books as I could get my hands on about weddings. But most of them dealt with the preparations for the bride and her family and what the groom needs to do and purchase. There was little information for the groom's mother. I came to feel that I was the least important person, but I was expected to show up.

The day of the weddings, we survived hurricanes and floods. I learned what to wear and what not to wear. I learned that it is important to have one's own support system. Do not go through this alone.

I learned so much through these experiences that I wanted to pass on my knowledge. I want other mothers who have a son about to get married to be better prepared than I was. That is why I wanted to write this book.

I put it off until recently. My sister-in-law, Linda, encouraged me to get started. She works in a major book store. One day a customer was looking for a book on weddings. Her son was getting married. Linda did not have anything to offer her, the mother of the groom. Hence, the next time I saw Linda, she said, "Hurry up and write the book. There is a demand for it." So now I have begun writing what has been on my mind for more than two years.

I hope you will enjoy this book, but most of all, I hope you will enjoy your son's wedding. If I can be of any help to just one person, it will have been worth the effort to write this book.

CHAPTER 1

DRESS TO IMPRESS

Grandma Mahood is a surrogate grandmother to my sons. She also belongs to the Eastern Star, which is part of the Masonic Lodge. They often have formal dress occasions, so she has many beautiful outfits. She often gives the clothes she no longer needs to me.

One day she gave me a beautiful light pink dress with matching jacket. It was a summer dress, knee length, with straps. It had a few rhinestones across the bodice. The jacket had 3/4 length sleeves, and also had rhinestones and pearls on the

1

lapels. It was beautiful and it fit me perfectly. So I told her, "I will wear this to the wedding of the first one of my sons to get married." She was pleased. So I kept the dress with this intention.

My youngest son, Erik, was the first to become engaged. He had been dating Nancy for six years. They had graduated from Cornell University the same year. So I already knew her and had met her family. They wanted to get married on the Cornell campus in one of the chapels there in the month of July.

After the holidays were over the winter before the wedding, we could concentrate on getting ready for the wedding. One day I called Nancy's mother in New York. I live in Oregon. I told her about the dress I wanted to wear to the wedding. I told her what color it was and why I wanted to wear it. She said that was okay with her. She said that she had not yet thought much about what she wanted to wear. So I was happy. I could wear the pink dress and jacket to Erik's wedding.

As it got closer to the wedding date, I decided I needed to have the dress dry cleaned. It had been many years since it had been worn, and I wanted it to look nice. So I took it to my favorite dry cleaner's. But they told me they could not dry clean it due to the rhinestones. The rhinestones would be ruined in the process of dry cleaning it. I was disappointed.

I was intent on having it cleaned, so I thought I would try to wash it. I used a mild soap and hand washed it in cold water. Then I hung it up to dry. It seemed to come out okay, but it needed ironing. So I ironed it. Then I tried it on. It had shrunk! Now I was really disappointed. There was no way I could wear it unless I lost at least 10 pounds. And I didn't think I could do that in one month.

So now I was back to square one. What was I going to wear to my son's wedding? I did not have enough time to make anything and do a decent job at it. So I began looking around in the stores. I discussed my dilemma with my co-workers. I went to the library to find out what was proper to wear. Black was out. Green was out (for some superstitious reason.) One of my co-workers told me that I was supposed to wear beige. Beige? That was no fun. I did not want to wear beige. She went so far as to loan me two beige dresses she had worn to her sons' wedding. But I did not want to wear them.

Since Nancy's mother seemed okay with me wearing the light pink, I decided I would try to find something else in that same color. I went from store to store, trying on everything I thought would work. I finally found a nice dress in a light pink. And it was very affordable. It had a knee length skirt. The top was the same color with short sleeves, and had a V-neck with a little white blouse insert. I thought it was perfect. I was very happy with my decision. I found shoes to match and I was ready to go.

I had informed my son of these events and I had told him about my new purchase. Neither he nor his fiancee said that it would not be okay, although by the tone of their voices, they did not sound totally pleased, either.

When I arrived in Philadelphia, where my son was living, I was anxious to show them my new outfit. They did not say much. They did not seem as excited about it as I was. I wondered why, but I did not suspect that I had committed a faux pas.

Prior to the wedding, all of the families of the happy couple spent a week on Cayuga Lake, next to the Cornell campus. So I had a chance to discuss the dress situation with the bride's mother. She told me about her dress; it was also light pink. She said that she had always wanted to wear pink to her daughter's wedding. Why had she not told me this before? I was shocked.

The day of the wedding, we were all in Ithaca, New York. I had my hair done in the morning. Even though hurricane Bertha blew through that day, my hair survived. The wedding was set to begin at 6:30. I got dressed and drove to the wedding with my son's step uncle, Bosco. He is the only one who seemed pleased with the way I looked.

Just before the wedding, we all congregated in the back of the chapel. When I saw what Nancy's mother was wearing, I gasped! She had on a beautiful long dress with a jacket. It must have been made with satin brocade. She looked lovely. But the color of her dress was the exact same color as mine! She did not say anything. But I had a feeling she was not pleased with me. She barely spoke to me the rest of the evening.

Everyone said I looked beautiful, and I had a good time, so I did not worry about the color of my dress too much. I figured people probably thought that we had planned on wearing the same color (sometimes the mothers do that.) But I had a lesson to learn here: WEAR BEIGE!

About a year later, my other son, David, announced that he and Rosemary were going to get married. They planned to get married in Austin, Texas in October. I think that part of the problem when Erik got married was that I lived so far away from him and the bride and her parents, that the communication was poor. If we had lived closer, I would have had a better idea what to wear and they could have told me whether my dress was going to be acceptable or not. So, especially, if you live a long distance from the happy couple, it is even more imperative to wear beige.

For David's wedding in Texas, I luckily, found a nice, simple dress and jacket in a catalog that was "champagne" color. There are so many shades of beige, from champagne to almost a brown. So that will give you more to choose from. Just make sure it is not white and not a dark brown. So I ordered my dress months before the wedding.

When the dress arrived, I was very pleased. It was simple and elegant, sleeveless with an empire waist, with satin bodice. The jacket was long with long sleeves, which, when folded up a bit, were satin. And it fit me perfectly! I found shoes to match that would be comfortable for dancing.

What I did not anticipate was gaining weight before the wedding. I gained about ten pounds, which now made the dress look tight on me. I needed to lose weight in order to get into the dress and not look sleazy for the wedding. And, if you are also in your 50's, like me, you know that it is not easy to lose weight!

Luckily, we began a weight loss program at work, so I had the support and competition of my fellow workers. But I did not lose all of the ten pounds. I lost enough to get into my new dress, but just barely. Since I was spending a week in Texas before the wedding, I had to be careful not to gain any more weight while I was there.

The day of the wedding finally came. Twin hurricanes blew up from Mexico through Austin, Texas. It was horrible. But the wedding went off as planned, even though it was questionable whether or not it would.

Again, I had my hair done the morning of the wedding. It survived the hurricanes, but came apart a little. That was okay, because it was a little over done. I barely had time to take a bath and get dressed, but we all arrived at the wedding on time, just as the sun broke through the clouds and it stopped raining. They were able to have the wedding outdoors, as planned. But they moved the reception indoors.

My sons told me I looked beautiful. I had my beige (champagne) dress and jacket on. I did not feel uncomfortable. No one could complain about what I was wearing. It was perfect.

Now you may be like me and think, "I do not want to wear beige!" But, believe me, you will be happier in the long run if you do. This is your son's wedding. Probably he and his bride are paying for it, if not her parents. You want them to be happy. You want them to be happy with you. This is not your wedding. As much as you might not want to yield to their wishes, if you want harmony in the family, you must do what you can to make them happy.

I have included a photo of myself with my son at his wedding on the cover. I am wearing the champagne dress. You can see that I found a very nice dress in that color.

I have been looking in catalogs and in department stores ever since. I have seen some beautiful dresses in beige, or shades close to beige. They would all be perfect to wear to your son's wedding. Just make sure the color is not so light that it looks white. You don't want your daughter-in-law to be angry with you for the rest of your life.

One of the things I learned is that you must have your shoulders covered. However, if the wedding is in the heat of the summer, you may want to wear something with just shoulder straps. But I would recommend a jacket to go with it to wear during the ceremony and the receiving line. After that, you can take off the jacket for the reception and dancing if you feel too warm. Some of the dresses I have seen have jackets that go with them.

Also, it depends upon the formality of the occasion. Some weddings call for a long, formal dress, while others are less formal. It is a good idea to check with the mother of the bride, if possible, or the bride, to to find out what their expectations are.

I have a few other suggestions regarding dressing for the wedding. Try on all of your clothes at least a week before the wedding. Be sure the shoes are comfortable. You will be in them for hours. Be sure the dress still fits you and that you have not gained weight, like I did.

Be sure the nylons fit. One of my friends did not try on her shoes and nylons ahead of time. The day of the wedding, she tried them on, and they did not fit. She had to wear an old pair of shoes without nylons to her son's wedding with her beautiful new dress!

I also suggest having your hair done professionally the morning of the wedding. I did this both times. But I would suggest making your own appointment. At my first son's wedding, I made my own appointment, letting them know ahead of time what I wanted and what the occasion was. It was a very relaxing experience, and I loved the way my hair turned out.

For my second's son's wedding, my future daughter-in-law made the appointment because I did not know where to go. When I arrived for my appointment, the hairdresser was upset because she did not know that I was the mother of the groom and she wanted my long hair done up very nicely. She hurried to get it done, even though it took her two hours. I was worried that I would not make it to the wedding on time. She was stressed and so was I. So, be sure you talk to the hairdresser yourself ahead of time so that she will be prepared.

Also, be sure to carry a nice hanky in your bag. If you are like me, you will cry at your son's wedding, not because you are losing your son, but because you will be so happy for him. I, also, bought a hanky for the mothers of the brides, as a little remembrance from me. While I was in Pennsylvania I visited the Amish country and found some beautiful hand made hankies. Every time I look at mine now, it brings back happy memories of the weddings.

Also be sure to have a nice, small handbag to carry your hanky in along with some necessities such as lipstick, powder, or tranquilizers. You do not want to be encumbered with a large bag while you dance and socialize. And you want it to match your lovely beige outfit that you are going to wear. Everyone will be impressed how beautiful and put together you look.

CHAPTER 2

GIFTS

Even though you may be spending hundreds or thousands of dollars to help out with the wedding, it is important to also give your son and his bride a wedding present. You do not want to give them a set a towels, or something someone else might give them. You want to give them something special; something they will always remember.

When my youngest son got married, I wanted to give him $1500.00. I thought they could use the money for the honeymoon, or something like that. But he told me they did not need the money. He wanted me to buy them something from Oregon. So I tried to think of something from Oregon that would cost that much money.

We have myrtlewood trees in Oregon from which beautiful gifts are made. I found one store that made furniture with the myrtlewood. It is very expensive, but I wanted something special for my son and his wife. I took photos of the furniture from the store and sent them to the happy couple. I wanted them to be pleased with the purchase. They chose a beautiful entertainment center. The store had it delivered to their home in Santa Barbara, California. They were very happy with the gift.

The main point I want to make is that it is okay to ask the couple what they would like to receive.

Since you want your gift to be very special, you want them to be happy with it. Therefore, asking them what they would like helps to ensure this.

When my second son got married, I sent them $7,000.00. I owed him this as he had helped me get through college. Therefore, he did not expect anything else from me. The $7,000.00 was going to help pay for the wedding. But I still wanted to purchase something.

They had registered for china and silver at a major department store. Since the settings are expensive, I knew they would not receive many complete place settings. Therefore, I purchased some china for them and some silver. They were happy with that as it gave them enough to use for their first Thanksgiving dinner that year.

Of course, this all depends upon how much money you have to spend. Some people can afford thousands of dollars, whereas others may only be able to afford a hundred dollars. I just suggest that you take care to get them something very special that they will love and cherish.

Another thing that is fun to do is to watch your son and his new wife open presents the morning after the wedding. Of course, this depends upon whether or not they have already taken off on their honeymoon, and if they are going to open presents. Etiquette dictates that people are not to bring presents to the wedding. But the reality of it is that they do.

When my first son got married, I had made airplane reservations to fly home early the next morning. I realized afterwards that it was a mistake. One reason is because I was exhausted. Making a cross country flight when you are exhausted is not a good idea. Also, it was a mistake because I missed the party the next day and I missed seeing them open presents.

So, when my next son got married, I intentionally made my airplane reservations two days after the wedding to fly home. The day after the wedding, several of us met at a favorite restaurant for breakfast. It was fun and casual and we all had a good time.

Then my brother, Jim, and I went over to my new daughter-in-law's parents' house to watch the couple open presents. It was a casual and intimate time we shared together. I will never forget it. After that, my brother and I went to a sports bar to watch a football game. It was a great day. When I flew home the next day, I was rested and in a good mood.

Of course, you need to ask the happy couple if it is okay for you to spend that time with them the day after the wedding. If they feel it is an invasion of their privacy, then you need to respect their wishes. But if it is possible, it is fun to watch them open the present or presents you carefully chose

for them.

CHAPTER 3

INVITATIONS

The bride and groom will be sending out the invitations. Usually, her parents will be helping with the expense of the wedding. Therefore, it is up to the bride and groom to put on the invitations whatever they want.

When my youngest son got married, I was hoping that my name would be included on the invitation. When I received my copy of the invitation in the mail, it was not. I was disappointed, but I did not make a fuss over it. My son informed me that Nancy's parents were paying quite a bit of money for the wedding. Therefore, they had the right to have the invitations printed the way they wanted.

The important lesson here is that it is your son's and his bride's wedding. They can do it any way they want. Even if you are paying for part of the wedding, if your name is not on the invitation, or, if they decide to do anything else you do not like, it is much more classy not to get upset with them. Cry if you must. Complain to your friends. Eat a box of chocolates or drink a glass of wine. But, please, do not ruin the wedding for the happy couple by getting upset over the decisions they make.

This also applies to who they wish to invite to the wedding. It is up to them to decide how many people they want to invite and who. It is not up to you. But, usually, you are allowed to have some say about inviting some of your friends and family.

Erik asked me months before his wedding who I would like to invite. I began by asking him how many people I could include on the guest list and went from there. I started with my family and then included some of my friends who had known him most of his life. Even if I knew they could not make the trip to the wedding, some people appreciated receiving an invitation. I actually asked my friends if they wanted an invitation.

They did not appear to be offended by this. I did not want to send an invitation to someone and then have them feel they needed to send a gift. Therefore I only included those people who really wanted an invitation. And some of them actually made the trip all the way across the country.

When my niece got married, my sister-in-law did not think of the fact that the groom's parents might want to make a list of people to invite. So if you are not asked who you may invite, do not be shy about bringing up the subject. There will be many people in your life who will be thrilled to share this happy occasion with you.

One regret I have is that I did not invite any of my cousins to my first son's wedding. I wanted to draw the line somewhere, so I did not include them.

But I realized later that they would have liked to have been invited. Therefore when my second son got married, I invited some of my cousins. A couple of them actually came and we had a good time. It was like a family reunion.

Another thought I have regarding this matter is the issue of inviting single people. My personal feeling is that if you are inviting a single person, especially if they will not know many people at the wedding, address the invitation with, "And Guest." Of course, this is your son's wedding, so it is up to him and his bride. But when I made out my list of whom to invite, I requested that single people be allowed to bring a guest.

I received an invitation to a wedding yesterday in the mail. I was expecting it and knew when the date was to be. I am a single person. I do not want to go to this wedding alone. A friend of mine would like to accompany me as he also knows the bride and the groom. But the invitation was only addressed to me. So now I am in a quandary as to what to do. Do I just go by myself? Do I call the bride and ask her if it is okay to bring my friend? I hate to do that as I know that she is probably very busy getting ready for the wedding. Do I just put down "2 guests" when I RSVP? I do not know what to do. So, see how much easier it would have been if they had invited me and a guest?

Therefore, include those people you want to share the happy occasion with. But be sure to check with your son and his fiancee before you make any final decisions. And do not get upset or show that you are upset if your name is not on the invitation.

CHAPTER 4

THE REHEARSAL DINNER

I have a difficult time understanding why people get upset over who is invited to the rehearsal dinner. One of the rules of etiquette states that the groom's family pays for the rehearsal dinner. If they are paying for the dinner, I would think that they could invite anyone they choose. But some brides and grooms think that only certain people can attend the rehearsal dinner. Times change, and rules change also, so it is okay to bend the rules.

My first son to get married, Erik, was married in New York. People were invited from all over the country. The families and the wedding party spent the week before the wedding in cabins along the Cayuga Lake in Ithaca, New York.

I am divorced from my sons' father and he has remarried. But we agreed ahead of time how to pay for the rehearsal dinner. My son wanted the rehearsal dinner to be next to the cabins on the lake. There was a large grassy area where we set up tables and chairs and canopies, in case it rained. My son knew that Hurricane Bertha was on its way, so he wanted to be prepared, just in case.

Around 6:00 in the evening, those who were in the wedding party went to the chapel on the

Cornell campus as we rehearsed the wedding. It was beautiful. I cried more there than at the wedding. Then we all went back to the cabins for the rehearsal dinner.

My son's father and his wife and I each paid one third for the dinner. My son had arranged everything: the tables, canopies, chairs, and the food at the local market. We just needed to pick everything up, pay for it, and take it to the cabins. I went with my former husband, his wife, and my mother to the store to do this. I was anticipating a very stressful shopping trip. But everything went great. We had a nice time. There were no quarrels and no stress.

We also had invited to the dinner everyone who had already arrived for the wedding, which meant about 60 people. There were relatives, some who were in the wedding and some who were not. There were friends who had traveled all the way across the country to join my son and his bride to be for this happy event. We felt it was only right to include them.

We all had a wonderful time. We even had food left over. It was a grand party. My only regret was that I spent so much time socializing with everyone that I did not help with the cooking (bar-b-q.) My former husband and his wife did most of the work. I went around visiting everyone. But I felt that was my job also. It was wonderful.

Two years later, my other son, David, got married in Austin, Texas. That is where his wife is from and where her parents live. Months before the wedding, her parents decided to have their house remodeled. They wanted to have the rehearsal dinner at their house and they wanted it to look nice.

Rosemary's parents had a room added onto their house. Her grandfather had been a minister and Rosemary's mother had inherited some of the stained glass windows from his church. Since she is an artist, she designed and put the pieces of glass together to put up in this new room. I was there when the window was installed. It was beautiful.

They also had new hardwood floors put in throughout the house. Since I spent a couple of nights at their place before the wedding, and since I was partly responsible for the rehearsal dinner, I spent the day vacuuming and dusting the floors. I also cleaned all the new windows in the new room. Three whole sides of the room are all window, so I spent a great deal of time doing this. But I was happy to do it, since they had, graciously, volunteered to have the dinner at their house.

Again, there were about 50 people at the rehearsal dinner. We invited everyone who had already arrived from all over the country, not just people in the wedding party. My son grew up in California and Oregon, attended a university in

Massachusetts, and was stationed in the Navy in Florida and Washington. Rosemary had lived in Seattle, Washington, and in Alaska. So they had friends all over the country. Since their friends had traveled so far, we could not possibly exclude them from the rehearsal dinner party.

We spent the day of the rehearsal dinner fixing up the house. The food and beverages had already been ordered. That had all been arranged ahead of time. We just needed to go to the store, pick them up, and take them to the place of the rehearsal dinner.

Around 5:00 that evening we went to the Oasis, where the rehearsal took place for the wedding. There were people at the rehearsal who were not in the wedding party, such as my mother. It was a beautiful evening. The sun was shining and we all wore summer clothes on this October evening. The Oasis sits on Lake Travis in Austin, Texas. We relaxed outdoors, over-looking the lake, as we watched the rehearsal. None of us anticipated the hurricane that was to hit the next day.

After the rehearsal, we returned to Rosemary's parents' house. Everything was set up and ready. The house was packed full of happy people. The food was wonderful. It was a grand party. Everyone had a wonderful time. But, like the other wedding rehearsal dinner, I spent so much time visiting with people, that I was not much help in the kitchen. Rosemary's aunt and uncle did much of the work. But no one complained to me about it. I had helped to get the house ready, so I assumed that made up for it.

The day after the wedding, which took place, in spite of the twin hurricanes, a group of us met at a restaurant in Austin for breakfast. It was mostly family who stayed over one more day. My son and his bride had not left on their honeymoon yet, so they joined us. We had a wonderful, fun time.

My former husband approached me about the cost of the wedding rehearsal dinner. I told him that I had already given our son and his wife $7,000. At first, he did not believe me, but I convinced him that it was true. My son had not expected me to pay anything extra for the rehearsal dinner or anything else.

I was sitting across from my former husband and his wife at breakfast that morning. I listened to him inform his wife that they owed David and Rosemary $14,000! Since I had paid $7,000, he said they each also owed $7,000. Of course, he was only joking. I do not know how he settled with David or Rosemary's parents. It would have been nice if he could have helped with the remodeling of the house. But there were no resentments. Everyone was happy.

My niece got married this past year. The wedding took place in the city where her parents live in Washington. The groom's parents came all the way from Michigan. They had planned to pay for the rehearsal dinner. It was to be at a restaurant. I was invited because I was considered a member of the wedding since I was going to play the piano at the ceremony.

As with my sons' weddings, people were coming from all over the country to attend the happy event. Some would be arriving the day before the wedding. My sister-in-law, the bride's mother, felt she was responsible for providing dinner for all the people who were not invited to the rehearsal dinner. So her plan was to prepare some food and they could stay at her house and eat while the rest of us were at the rehearsal and the rehearsal dinner. I thought this was, perhaps, too much for her to do, but she felt an obligation to help out.

The day before the wedding, I picked up my son and my cousin at the Portland, Oregon airport. Then we drove four hours to get to the place of the wedding, in Kennewick, Washington. We stopped along the way to eat at a restaurant, and I used my cell phone to call them and let then know we were on our way. I am glad I did, because there had been a change in plans.

The groom's family decided that everyone would be invited to the rehearsal dinner who had already arrived for the wedding. It was to be held at a Chinese restaurant and there would be plenty of room to seat everyone in the banquet room.

When we arrived at my brother's house, we barely had time to greet them, get to the hotel and check in and then get to the church for the rehearsal. But we made it on time. Everyone was at the church, watching, whether they were in the wedding or not. It was fun.

After the rehearsal, we all found our way to the Chinese restaurant. There were tables set up for all of us in the banquet room. They fed us several courses of delicious food. It was wonderful. We all had a good time. I don't think the groom's parents minded paying for the dinner for so many people. I never heard them complain.

But, perhaps, you are not paying for the dinner. Perhaps you cannot afford it. Perhaps your son and his bride are paying for it and they cannot afford one more person. I think that one needs to consider that money is not the most important thing in this world. The feelings of those we love are more important. I would recommend doing what makes your son and his bride happy and as many other people happy as possible.

My point is that etiquette states that the groom's parents pay for the rehearsal dinner. If they are paying for it, I think they may invite whoever they want to invite. It does not have to be for just the people in the wedding party. And the rehearsal dinner can be anywhere. Etiquette changes with time. This is one part of the wedding that is changing. Be flexible. Have a good time.

And try to make sure that everyone else has a good

time too.

CHAPTER 5

MUSIC AND DANCING

Erik was the first one of my sons to get married. Music has been a large part of both of our lives. My mother had been a music major in college. Both my brothers and I studied music. One of my brothers received his degree in music composition. I made it a point to have my sons study music. Erik chose to be the singer.

Since music is so important to us, Erik wanted to be sure that the music was perfect for his wedding. One day when I was talking to him on the phone, he asked me what music I wanted played as dance music at his wedding and what song I wanted for us (he and I) to dance to. I thought this was very considerate of him to ask me what I wanted.

When he was in high school, he was in many musical productions. One of the songs performed while he was the groom, was "Sunrise, Sunset," from Fiddler on the Roof. I had always thought that it would be a perfect song for his wedding. So when he asked me the above question, I told him I wanted to dance to "Sunrise, Sunset" with him. My wishes were honored and I cherish the moment.

Not all sons are going to ask you what music you want played or what you want to dance to with him. But it may be something you want to think about, whether they ask you or not. If your son is not interested in music, or does not ask what your wishes are, then just let it go. But you could ask him.

Erik also had played a few other songs that I suggested. It was a wonderful wedding and reception. The dancing was so much fun. No one wanted to leave.

I had wanted to play the piano for them at the wedding. I do not play very well, but I wanted to make this contribution. But Erik did not want me to play for them. I am glad that he insisted I not play. I have learned that the mother of the groom is not there to perform or to contribute any other services (see the chapter, "You are not getting paid.") You are there to have a wonderful time and to enjoy your friends and family.

It is also a custom for the mother of the groom to dance with the father of the bride. But Nancy's father never asked me to dance. I did not want to press the matter, but my feelings were kind of hurt. I did not say anything to anyone about this, however.

When my second son, David, got married, Nancy's family (Erik's wife's family) was invited. Two years had passed since Erik's wedding. I got up the nerve to say to Nancy's father, jokingly, "You did not dance with me at Erik's wedding." He was totally oblivious to this or to the fact that he was supposed to. So at David's wedding, I danced with Erik's father-in-law. All was made well.

I guess the lesson here is that, even if someone hurts your feelings, do not say anything. Have a sense of humor and eventually, all will be made right.

But, if you can, dance with the bride's father! It is tradition. And be sure to dance with your son, to the music of your choice, if that is possible.

CHAPTER 6

YOU ARE NOT GETTING PAID

In the last chapter, I mentioned that I wanted to perform at my son's wedding. Mainly, I wanted to play the piano. I am glad I did not. The mother of the groom is not there to perform or to provide any other services.

You will be nervous as it is, getting up in front of hundreds of people, walking down the isle, with everyone looking at you. I started to hyperventilate walking down the isle at Erik's wedding. By the time David got married, it was a cinch.

One of my friends agreed to be the photographer at her son's wedding (a way to save money.) Later, she told me that she regretted it. She spent the whole time "working." She was not able to relax and enjoy the happy occasion. She was too busy taking photographs. Then she spent a great deal of time having the photos developed, putting them in an album and mailing them to the happy couple. This was very nice of her, but she said she would rather have relaxed and enjoyed the wedding.

One of my friends made a pillow for the ring bearer to carry down the isle. That is okay. You can do that ahead of time, if you wish. But do not feel under obligation to provide any services (except for the wedding rehearsal dinner.) You are not getting paid.

Also, if the couple wants you to cater the wedding, that is a request you need to turn down. Again, you will not have a good time at the wedding if you do this.

You want to have a wonderful, relaxing time at your son's wedding. Do not agree to do anything for which other people would get paid.

CHAPTER 7

YOUR OWN ATTENDANT

This is not something I learned from anything I read or from anyone else. It is something I learned from my own experience. You need to have someone there to support you. If you do not, you may find that you will crumble under the pressure.

If you are married, and your husband is very supportive, then you are lucky. He can be your support person. But not all of us are that lucky. So think of someone who will help you get through the wonderful day.

I am a single parent. When Erik got married, I was, basically, on my own. I was surrounded by family and friends, but no one was there the whole time to hold me up. When we finally arrived at the wedding, the stress became too much for me. After the wedding ceremony, I was ready to leave and not tell anyone where I was going. I could have done it. No one was watching me. But I took a deep breath and went back to the reception. I am glad I did. I ended up having a wonderful time. There was a special table for me and my family and my best friends for the sit down dinner. We ate, drank and danced and had a good time. It was wonderful. But I almost missed this special time. It scares me to think that I almost left.

When David got married, things were a little different. I shared a room with one of David's woman friends. Plus I stayed in a hotel where the rest of my family was staying.

My sister-in-law, Linda, and I were going to go for a walk along the river the morning of the wedding. She called me after we had breakfast and said that they were expecting seven inches of rain in the next few hours. So we canceled our plans. We decided to go to the mall across the street from our hotel room instead. So she, one of her daughters and my roommate went to the mall for awhile.

I also planned to have my hair done that day. I talked Linda into going with me to have her hair done also. It took a long time to get both of us looking great. When we were done, we walked out into the windy, hurricane air. We made it back to the hotel in time to get cleaned up and dressed. Then we car pooled to the wedding.

She, my brother and mother were in one car and I was in another with my cousins. Since the road to the wedding had been changed, due to the hurricane, I got lost. It turned out that I went 20 miles out of our way. So we stopped and my brother helped me figure out how to get to the wedding. We arrived just in time.

I do not know how I would have made it through that day without my sister-in-law helping me. It was so stressful, having to change plans due to the hurricane. I was stressed worrying that I would not make it to the wedding on time, let alone whether or not there was going to be a wedding. She was with me the whole time, keeping me calm. We made it to the wedding, and everything was wonderful.

My point here is that if you are planning to go to the wedding alone, do not be alone. Pick someone who you are close to who can be with you most of the day of the wedding. That person can make sure you are on track, that you do not lose your composure, that you look great, and that you show up. My brother said that fifty percent of life is just showing up. So have someone with you to make sure that you do show up and that you

have a wonderful time.

CHAPTER 8

HURRICANES, FLOODS AND OTHER

DISASTERS

Erik and Nancy were married in Ithaca, New York. It is a long distance inland from the Atlantic coast. Therefore, when the news was reported about Hurricane Bertha the week before their wedding, I did not worry. It was supposed to hit the Atlantic coast, but, surely, I did not think it would come inland. I had a lot to learn.

The morning of the wedding, I had my hair done. I was very happy with the results. There had been beautiful weather the whole week before, but that morning it was raining. I walked out of the beauty salon into the rainy weather. But I had my umbrella with me, and my hair held up.

I went to purchase a newspaper for that day. I wanted to save it and give it to Erik and Nancy for their first anniversary as a remembrance. I went to the section with the weather report. It said that Hurricane Bertha was to hit Ithaca, New York at 6:00 P.M. that day. The wedding was scheduled for 6:30! I began to panic.

I called Erik when I arrived back at the cabin. I told him the hurricane was to hit there that day. He said, "I know, Mom. I have been watching the weather reports all week. I just did not tell you because I did not want you to worry."

Gee, thanks a lot. Now I was really worried.

There were four weddings scheduled that day in the same chapel that Nancy and Erik were getting married in on the Cornell Campus. The first one was scheduled for 1:30.

Around 1:00 the rain started to let up. By 1:30 it had quit raining. It did not rain the rest of the day. Was this some kind of a miracle? Were people praying for it not to rain? I do not know. As it turned out, the hurricane came through that morning, which was the rain I experienced after I had my hair done. By the time Erik and Nancy's wedding took place, the sky was clear. It was a beautiful wedding and they were able to take photos outside after the ceremony. We all walked across the street to the hall where the reception was to be held. There was no hurricane; there was no rain. No one got wet and we all had a wonderful time.

David got married two years later in Austin, Texas. Their wedding was set for October 17th. It is not a good idea to have a wedding in the summer in Texas; it is too hot. October has nicer weather. But there is still the chance of a hurricane. I remember sitting in my daughter-in-law's mother's house in Austin a few days prior to the wedding. She said, "This time of year you always have the chance of having a hurricane." But the weather predictions looked good. We were not worried.

I spent the week prior to the wedding being a tourist in Texas, as I had never been there before. I drove to Nuevo Laredo by myself and went shopping. I drove back to San Antonio and spent the night there. The next morning I did the River Walk, saw the Alamo, and the other missions, and then drove back to Austin. The weather was gorgeous. I had a wonderful time by myself.

People slowly started arriving from all over the country for the wedding. We still had wonderful weather. There was no rain, and it was not too hot. But we kept watching the weather reports, just in case. They were predicting a storm through San Antonio, but then it was supposed to head up to Dallas, not Austin.

The evening before the wedding, we had the rehearsal at the Oasis, where the wedding was to be held. It was a beautiful evening. We all drove back to Rosemary's parents' for the rehearsal dinner. The weather was great, and we all had a wonderful time. No one had any idea of what we were to experience the next day.

My family was staying in the same hotel that I was. So the morning of the wedding, we all had breakfast downstairs together. It was fun. My sister-in-law, Linda, and I had made plans to go down to the lake and walk around it. Other people made plans to go shopping or go to the museum.

I went back to my room after breakfast. My sister-in-law called me. She said the news reported that there was a storm headed towards Austin. They were expecting seven inches of rain. We could not go walking down by the lake. I was very disappointed, but we decided to go to the mall across the street from the hotel, just to be safe.

My sister-in-law, my niece, my son's friend, Margueritte, and I went to the mall where we were able to keep dry and warm. After a couple of hours, we walked out into the wind and rain. We climbed into my rental car and started to head back to the hotel. The streets were already starting to flood. All of a sudden, I had a thought to go to my son's place. It was like my guardian angel was talking to me. So I turned right. There was a car in front of me, so I did not see the foot or more of water that I had to drive through until it was too late. I was worried that my brakes would get wet and we would have an accident. But the car was okay and we made it to my son's place.

We walked in the door and there was my future daughter-in-law in tears. The road to the Oasis was closed. My son was just sitting there, holding her, with a bewildered look on his face. He did not know what to do or say to comfort his beautiful bride to be. Rosemary, choking back the tears, said, "I just want to get married today."

Rosemary is five inches taller than me, but I took her in my arms and said, "You are going to get married today, even if you have to get married at your mother's house. Now dry your tears and get going." She needed to get to the hairdresser's. I asked her if there was anything we could do. We helped her get everything packed up in bags and got her out the door to the hairdresser's.

We went back to our hotel. There was still the problem of notifying people all over town that the road to the Oasis was closed and people had to take an alternate route. At our hotel, there were signs put up notifying people of the changes. David and Rosemary were not the only couple planning to get married that day. There were many weddings all over Austin. So people going to all the weddings needed to be notified of any changes. It was a nightmare.

Linda and I went to the hairdresser's to have our hair done. We returned in time to take a bath and get dressed.

Since my brother did not know how to get to the Oasis, he planned to follow me in the car he had rented. Three people were riding with him and three with me. I planned to take the alternate route since I did not know whether or not the main road had opened up.

Since I had not taken this route before, I got lost. We passed the turnoff. In Texas, the street signs are so small, which I don't understand because they boast of everything being the biggest in Texas. I had gone twenty miles out of our way before we stopped to try to figure out what had happened.

We turned around and went back the way we came. We found the turnoff. Now I was worried that we would be late for the wedding. I had been praying all day for the weather to clear up. About an hour before the wedding, it stopped raining. As we arrived at the Oasis, just in time, we noticed that there was a break in the clouds. The sun was trying to shine through. I felt my prayers had been answered.

We gathered outside for the wedding, as planned. It did not rain on us. Not everyone made it to the wedding, due to the weather. But about three quarters of the people showed up. We felt this was a miracle. The reception was moved indoors because it appeared it was going to rain again.

The wedding was a success. We all had a wonderful time and we have beautiful photos to prove that it turned out okay. Many people have stories to tell about their adventures trying to get to the wedding. But it was a very stressful day for all of us, especially for my son and his bride.

We found out the next day, from reading the newspaper, that twin hurricanes had blown up from the Pacific coast from Mexico. None of the weather people had predicted this. So no one had planned for it. There were several people killed in Austin that day. Sadly, some of the people who died were returning home after attending other weddings.

I like to think that there is never a perfect wedding. Something will go wrong. That way one can be prepared and not too disappointed when something does go wrong. And it will give everyone something to talk about and laugh about later. At David's wedding, the biggest problem was the weather. At Erik's wedding, the biggest problem was that he forgot to bring the guest book for everyone to sign. He had gone through a great deal of trouble trying to find just the right guest book, and then he forgot it. Oh, well, you can't expect everything to be perfect.

I oftentimes ask the members of the wedding afterwards if anything went wrong, suspecting that something must have happened that was not expected. But I am surprised how many people say that nothing went wrong. They, happily, say that it was a perfect wedding. Perhaps there is divine intervention. I do not know. But most weddings take place without any or with very few problems.

I think the main lesson I learned from my experiences is that the mother of the groom needs to be there and to be supportive of her son and his bride. When things start to go wrong, which they usually do, you need to be there to help out. You need to try to keep everyone calm, even if you are not. You need to try to make sure that the wedding still goes on as planned, even if there are hurricanes, floods, or other disasters.

CHAPTER 9

STEP FAMILIES, IN-LAWS AND OTHER

RELATIVES

I always find it difficult to understand how people find a way to ruin a happy occasion like a wedding by getting upset with other people. Somehow, it becomes important to bring up all the unhappy memories of the past and use the wedding as a stage to resolve conflicts. This is not a courtroom. It is a wedding, a very happy celebration. It is a time to set aside all of our differences, a time to forgive people for past mistakes, and to celebrate the union of two families.

I am divorced from the father of my two sons. He remarried and he and his wife have two other children. I have always encouraged my sons to have a very close relationship with all of them. So, of course, they were all a part of the wedding plans.

I have already mentioned that when Erik and Nancy got married in Ithaca, New York, we spent a whole week before the wedding on Lake Cayuga in cabins. Since I was alone, I needed to decide with whom I would stay. My son suggested I stay in the same cabin with his father and his family.

Some people would think that this would be an outrageous solution, but it worked out fine.

I arrived at the lake ahead of my son's father's family. So I had the cabin to myself. It was very relaxing. I could come and go as I pleased. I sat on the deck and sunbathed and read a book by myself.

When my son's father's family arrived, we all got along well. There were plenty of rooms for everyone. One day, my son's stepmother and I visited all of the wineries in the Finger Lakes region. We spent a whole afternoon doing this and had a wonderful time.

The day of the wedding rehearsal, we needed to get the food from the deli. I, my mother, my former husband and his wife all went in one car to the store. I was afraid it would be a fiasco, but that, too, worked out very well. The food was prepared ahead of time. We just needed to figure out where to pick it up and how to pay for it. There were no arguments and we really had fun.

I remember when my cousin's son got married. It was a large, lovely wedding. Our whole family was invited including both of my uncle's former wives (my uncle was deceased.) I was worried how everyone would get along, but that too worked out great. I think we were all so happy to see each other again after so many years that all the unpleasant memories from the past were forgotten.

It is also important to try to make friends with your new in-laws. That can be difficult if the two families are of different cultures, backgrounds, or religions. But it is worth making the effort to get along and build a relationship that will last into the future.

One thing I did at both of my sons' weddings was to purchase a pretty hanky for each of the mothers of the brides. I knew I would need one myself if and when I got teary eyed. I figured they would need one also. Now each time I go to a wedding, I bring along the same pretty hanky I bought for myself. It brings back happy memories of my sons' weddings.

I live in Oregon and one of my son's in-laws' families lives in New York and the other in Texas. So we do not see each other very often. But I keep in touch with the family in Texas by e-mail. Recently, my newest granddaughter was put in the hospital when she was only six weeks old. I was as anxious as I have ever been in my life, worrying about her. Since I am friends with her other grandparents, who live near her, I felt comfortable calling them on the telephone to see how things were. I also appreciated the updates from them via e-mail regarding her progress and what was really going on. She is well now. But it made me realize how important it is for me to have that relationship with my son's in-laws.

Also, when she was born, I received a beautiful card from my other son's mother-in-law congratulating me. It was the only card I received of congratulations on her birth, so that card meant a great deal to me.

It will become more apparent after you have grandchildren how important it is to build these relationships. But it needs to begin now, if you have not already made friends with your son's future in-laws.

The second most important relationship you need to build at this time is with your new daughter-in-law. That could be the subject of a whole other book, one I do not feel equipped to write. But some of the things you need to do or not do are fairly obvious.

The most important thing is to never criticize your new daughter-in-law, either to your son or to her or her family. Obviously, you will alienate her if you criticize her to her face and you will alienate your son if you do so to him. And it will not help to build a friendship with her family if you let them know of your complaints. If she does do something that drives you crazy, you have your own family or friends or therapist you can discuss that with. It is a much healthier approach to take.

Gifts are important. If you do not know what to purchase for her, you can ask her family or your son what would make her happy. Or you could find out what her favorite color is and purchase something for her in that color.

But all of this begins the day your son is born. It has been said that a son marries a woman just like his mother. So if you want your son to marry a nice girl, you need to be the nicest mother you can be. If you succeeded in that department, you should have no problems with your new daughter-in-law.

Of course, the most important relationship you need to develop is with your son. I know you will say that you have been developing that relationship all of his life. But things are going to be different from now on. Be prepared.

After Erik got married, I called him one day to chat with him. He said, "Now, you know Mom. I am a married man now. I cannot have the close relationship I had with you before."

I tried to be understanding. I wanted his marriage to be happy and to succeed. So I did not argue the point. But things turned out much differently than I expected.

My son went right into graduate school after he got married. His wife is a consultant, so she travels everywhere. She was gone most of the week. It worked out well for them because he could study during the week when she was gone. But my son still became lonely during the week. So who did he call? His mother, me. After he got married, I felt closer to him than before.

So if you feel threatened about losing your son when he gains a wife, try to be patient and understanding. It may turn out better than you expected. And when those wonderful grandchildren come along, they will really want your time and attention. The patience you display now will pay off in the long run. The relationships that you build on now will carry you through all of the happy, and not so happy, events of the future. It will be worth the effort you put into building happy relationships at the wedding.

CHAPTER 10

THANK-YOU'S, PHOTOS, ETC.

I am sure you are thinking that you do not need to be concerned about thank-you's. That is the concern of the bride and groom. But I think that you will find you are concerned after the wedding.

Many mothers of the groom are worried that the bride will not send thank-you's, or will not send proper ones. I was fortunate in that both my daughters-in-law sent very nice thank-you's to everyone. One of them sent a professional photo with each one. But not every daughter-in-law is that considerate.

My cousin was very upset when her daughter-in-law sent a generic thank-you to everyone. There was no mention of the type of gift received. My cousin tried to make up for it first by apologizing, then my extending her thanks to everyone she knew.

I realize that it would not be proper for you to send thank-you notes to everyone in the absence of your daughter-in-law and son sending them, but you can apologize and thank them personally if this occurs.

I found that I wanted to personally thank my friends and family who I had invited. So when I had my photos developed, I sent them one or two, especially if I had a photo with them in it, and thanked them for making the trip to the wedding. I think that this was okay to do.

Another thing I did was to thank the ministers who performed the ceremonies. Again, I sent them each a photo with them in it with the happy couple. I thanked them for performing a lovely ceremony. Of course, this is not necessary. I just wanted to do it because both of the wedding services my sons were in were very nice and I felt the ministers had gone out of their way to make them special.

Now that I have mentioned photos, I would like to say a word or two about them.

I am a compulsive photographer. My son makes fun of me because I always have my camera with me and I feel a need to take photos of everything. I call myself "The Family Historian."

Therefore, when my sons got married, I wanted to have my own camera with me to take photos. But I thought it would look tacky for the mother of the groom to go around taking photos of the wedding. What was I to do?

At the rehearsals, I brought my camera. Everyone was dressed casually, so it did not look out of place for me to be carrying my camera and taking photos. I was able to get some wonderful photos of everyone and of the scenery and of the chapel. I knew I would not be able to take these photos the day of the wedding.

When I was escorted down the isle on the happy day, I could not carry a camera. It would have looked out of place. So I did not carry one at all during the wedding ceremonies. But I did go to my car and get my camera after the ceremonies were over. At first, I felt self conscious and uncomfortable, taking photos of everyone, or having someone take photos of me with the guests and bride and groom. But about half the people brought their own cameras anyway, so no one thought anything of the fact that I brought my camera and took some photos. As it turned out, some of my photos came out better than the ones the professional photographers had taken. So I am very happy that I did take my camera, and I think my sons and their wives are also. Therefore, I think it would be okay if you wanted to bring a camera and take photos also. Just do not do so during the ceremony. Let the professional do that.

Some brides and grooms place little disposable cameras on the tables for people to take candid photos. This works out very well also. You can just pick up one of those and take photos, and no one will think a thing of it.

Probably the most awkward thing to think about is what you want your new daughter-in-law to call you. My sons' friends had always called me, "Mom," or "My Other Mom." So I just expected my daughters-in-law to call me, "Mom" also. But it did not turn out that way.

93

Both of them call me Jane, which is my first name. I have never known whether or not to suggest something different. I figure if they wanted to call me something different, they would. But that is up to you. You may want to talk to them about it, or it may come naturally. You may want them to call you, "Mrs. Smith," but I doubt it. This is the one thing I do not have an answer to. You need to do what is best for your situation and your family.

As time passes, customs change and therefore, etiquette changes. The things that were important to remember and to do fifty years ago are not the same today and will not be the same in another ten or twenty years. So if you want to change customs and do things differently, that is okay. Or if your wonderful son and his beautiful bride want to do things differently, that is okay also.

I think the most important things to remember before, during, and after the wedding are to be flexible, be happy, and have a wonderful time. If you keep these in mind, everything will turn out great.

If things do go well, you may be lucky enough to receive a beautiful thank-you note, like the one I received:

"Dear Mom,

Thank you very much for all of our beautiful wedding presents, and for our funny cards and our beautiful card, and

95

especially for helping make the whole shindig possible. Everyone said how nice you were, and how beautiful you looked— we just said, 'We know.' It was great having you out for the week; it made me enjoy my last single week a lot more. Thank you again so very much.

Love,

Rosemary and David"

A NOTE TO THE READER

I am sure that not all of you will agree with what I have written, and that is okay. Times change, etiquette changes, and people change. Plus people are all different. You really can do things any way you want to. I just wanted to write this book for those of you who have questions about how to prepare for your son's wedding. I still recommend reading some etiquette books to get you started. But I thought that this would help you to get some ideas from someone who has been there.

If you would like to make any comments, send me questions, or share your ideas and solutions to your son's wedding day problems, I would be happy to hear from you . My e-mail address is SABATINOJANE @aol.com. I hope everything goes well and I hope you have a wonderful time at your son's wedding. And I hope this book has helped you in some way.

Jane Sabatino

Mother of the Groom

Jane Sabatino

About the Author

Jane Sabatino lives in Salem, Oregon. She raised her two sons in southern Oregon. They went away to college, and subsequently, met and married women from other states. One wedding took place in New York and the other in Texas. Jane was able to combine two of her hobbies, photography and writing, to create a delightful book about these experiences.